ETCHING THE GHOST

ETCHING THE GHOST

POEMS

CATHLEEN COHEN

atmosphere press

TABLE OF CONTENTS

IF RELEASED, MAGNIFICENT

WEIGHT OF THE PRESS

NO MISTAKES IN ART

AS WITNESS, AS ECHO

IF RELEASED, MAGNIFICENT

SOME TIDE

skimming air,

each stroke, a note
carried, counted and lit.

I need most
what I can't control,

each stroke with a squirrel tail brush
dipped in watercolor,

each hand jitter, each twitch,

jagged petals
more thorn than rose.

There's no covering up,
no layers of thick, embodied oil paint
to dissemble.

This flower looks carved in quartz,
says my son, frowning,
tilting it up to light.
Where's this from?

A garden
            I can't name

but my hand meant it,
the brush, vibrations, some tide
flung out in the wind.

IMAGE

hovers at 2:00 am,
whines for pigment, pulls me

onto a cold floor, reaching for brushes.

It needs fingers, a fleet wrist
that snaps over prey.

Sky lightens. I float
shimmery washes, a dash
down the brush,
                 graphite scurry, the line

sketching itself.

PANORAMA

I'm trying to paint this landscape
without myself in it

as I was taught
to be impartial,
to seek a clear view.

It's fine to circle a field or park
before unpacking the easel, but don't
spend hours on this.

Just receive panorama.

Light will change.
Given time, forms contract
or bleed into each other.

Take this birdfeeder,
slash of black pole signaling
trees to stay rooted.
It points at storm clouds, unmoved

until they move,
allowing sun to bake the surround.
Now this slim pole is

less confident, less focused.
It rolls out in the bleached grass and naps.

I brush dark tones and light,
locate the bones before they shift

to mower drone, childhood lawns, swooping

on bikes, calling out to my sisters in codes,
racing stop signs and lights, stubbing
tires on curbs, falling off.

Springing up.
Brushing layer on layer, the plunge
from the schoolyard slide, can't catch

my breath, just

lay there
with only sky blaring
cobalt blue
                glints and shards

I can't obscure
with brushstrokes of soft ochre grass

or anything bucolic.

TETHER

In art school we sketch
a red-tailed hawk
rescued from a park and nursed

but still
      unfit for soaring.

Each week he arrives, cinched
to his handler.

Any promise of wind sets him off
as he scans
      where we statue ourselves,

attempt to hide in space
he could breach with spectacular speed
              if released,
magnificent, earth-toned, heaving

one who ignores us
in search of egress.

2.

Leap
    down steps

to chalk games, stickball, *A my name*
inventing each day
               we circle and swoop.

Packs form and scatter.

We shun the boy
who rips wings off bees,
the girl who tells secrets.

Mothers (bright laughter, red lips)
clump together on curbs,
                sipping whisky
in paper cups.

3.

Possibly wind

fans us out past dark.
Fathers shout our names from doorways.

In hedges we crouch,
plan forays and small rebellions.

I tear my yellow dress
in a dirt fight, then lie

to my mother's shocked face.

4.

We were

feathered, colorful,
jittery, seeking
            escape.

Those long days, those years
bound together, we scanned

skies and airflow,
our fingers
            poised at doorknobs then

dropped.

5.

Each time sketching the hawk,
I'm entranced

by his handler, a young
woman who grasps
his cage and leather strap.

Not losing composure, she coos
when he panics,
produces a flute to lull him

to calm
as he shudders
calms
shudders.

6.

My first solo show
features birds of prey:

owls, peregrine falcons,
red tails in flight   or grasping
mice and starlings.

Frenzy of shadows, feathers,
talons.

Family and friends attend
(a good crowd)

but no one asks.

VOICE

If air shatters
into fault lines and shards

I will reach
to collect what flies out
                          and give voice.

I will echo
the glitter, the sharpness.

OPTICS

Camera obscura,

box of mirrors
blurring:

elbow
draped over a stool,
pears in a blue bowl, forsythia
cuttings. We take turns

peering through a single lens.
Hazy vision. Unwieldy
box with its cyclops eye.

Most turn away, annoyed
but I love distortions, how
color concentrates and deepens.

I stare so hard
that apples on a cloth merge
into ochre and crimson,
saturation with no

narrative, no words.

GLAZE

Into landscapes I scratch
messages
             so faint

no one detects clots of umber, bruise blue
below shimmer.

This is how watercolor can behave,
offering layers of glaze
                          so arresting

you're lost
             in its prisms, distracted

from what's beneath:
shocked eyes.

GREEN

I.

I was the girl in the passenger seat. Sap
green girl   with an older boy in a red car,
speeding.

Think of creatures with limbs like deer,
electric hair, thrill of summer heat,
hairpin turns, foliage, just racing through
landscape with no

witnesses.

2.

And only story

later, my story
           not his.

What is talk?
His voice, a stream
lulls in the flickering wind and

I'm caught
           in a green, winding drive to a grand stone
house.
He hooks my arm, steps us in
to greet his parents, who are oddly

still, leached of color, like in old photos.

Don't they recognize their son?
They seem startled by this

rift in the afternoon
then nod slightly at me,
                green girl, sapling, barely
camouflaged.

Years later, I think
this is the moment
           I should have dimmed myself.

3.

We climb the back stairwell
past a second floor and up
to a third flight. He prattles,

propels us through a maze of rooms, making
jokes with no sense, narrates:
the den, bedrooms, attic

and the next two images are linked,
in the washroom alone
                    and with him.

Crowding out most of the frame: his neck,
thick arms
            twisting us both in a knot I can't
unknot

fingers useless, skittering

no rewind, no turn back, no
windows spring open
                    with my cries.

No safety below, just
limbs and roots, detritus, clotted trees
and downstairs?

Only that family
            like fog, dispersing.

4.

You could ask   how I

let him
        drive me home later
in that smooth, purring car.

Shadows flicker across windshield, steering wheel, his
wrists, my
            lap.

Shadow, light, shadow,
rhythmic like breath, like

evidence
        I'm still in my body.

5.

He's joking again, but
a voice says
                don't.

Possibly my voice.

Radio static. I won't
recall
what songs drifted into the night, only

hands flexing.

6.

Some clichés are true.

Clothes shed, mirror stare, shock
at few visible signs.

No arm bruises, just
cover up the neck.

The shower cliché is true.

Merciful sting
sluices shame
                for a moment, then

must shower again
and again and again and again and again and again.

7.

Shift
        to a form
that moves among others

but hardly sits or eats.

In a hectic family it's possible

not to notice refusal
                    to speak
                    or lift a ringing phone.

My stiffening tongue.

8.

That spring, my brother's ninth-grade friend was jumped in the bushes. A fierce girl, she cut school and traipsed through town, enlarging her circumference. Battles with her mother were legendary, red storm clouds swept down the block as they shrieked.

One night she set out alone to a party. He had a record, we learned later.

She made a statement then went to live out of state with an uncle until the trial. Her house became a husk, her mother rarely spoke.

EVERY ROOM

Disguised for a long time, I was
skittish   *SQUIRREL!*
sensitive to air shifts,
                    whatever entered a room.

I grew hair long
                    to curtain neck and shoulders.
Camouflage   *LIZARD!*
baggy skirts, color of stone.

Flitted through conversation.
No one asked   *FINCH!* why I
pecked at food, swiveled eyes
upward.

Even now, I locate
every window and door in every room
I enter.

WEIGHT OF THE PRESS

ETCHING THE GHOST

Inking a copper plate will yield
a rich intaglio print
under the weight of the press.

You ink again and print again
fifty times, a hundred,
completing the run.

But the plate, though degraded
will hold enough ink in its teeth
to print a ghost.

This ghost is changed,
an imprint not true
to the image

you've scratched into copper,
permanently pocked
with grooves of dark and light.

This ghost is blurred,
a less wan sister
and wilder flurry.

LIFE CLASS

We maneuver easels
to circle a chair raised on blocks

like a throne
where the model will sit, but

she's not here, lost
on another floor?

For fifty long minutes her absence
is a living presence.

Our instructor swoops about, flinging
tidbits: *Squeeze out*

a palette of lead white, black, ocher, vermillion.
That's all the Masters had,

that's all you need, so little,
just a willingness to sit
with the topography of a face.

We prime our canvases, catch
the light that caresses
her face when she comes.

Here will be her brow.
Here, her orbital eminences.

We position our easels like steeds.
Someone elbows me
out of the sight line. No matter.

I'm transfixed by our teacher,
gaunt like a Renaissance figure.

Finally, the model arrives, gleaming
into this dark space.
Mounting steps, she is wordless,
unapologetic.

Up jumps our instructor, adjusts spotlights
to enhance the cream of her skin. We begin

to cough, scratch frantic brushwork,
eye her cheekbone, the distance
from her hairline to chin.

Rembrandt and van Eyck
lick their brush points,
judge the exact chroma of her flesh.

I covet their secrets, strive
to render this.

STUDIO

Someone slants a light, unfurls
red silk across a table.

Cabbages, cracked mirrors,
green onions in a bowl, gleam.

We are rich, possessed of
high windows, good light and all this time.

Outside, trucks gear and groan but
we are buffered by amber glaze.

Everything emerges after brushwork and scraping:
interiors, baby dolls, my brother's face.

We break on piles of rags and old brocades.
Jittery hands, coffee cups.

It can get obsessive.
Some labor all night and rouse to take up the brush.

Some see God in this - harmonious lines, golden triangles.
Some paint the same landscape day after day.

I watch dust drift, tender gestures of a wrist, cerulean
carefully placed.

Tonight our thighs will be
blue volumes tangled in onionskin.

STEALING COLORS

for Seymour Remenick

It's wrong to steal another's colors

but, lured
by the flicker of light in his landscapes,

I copy my teacher's list:
raw sienna, vermillion, sour manganese   jumping
from brickworks to the river. They swirl
and are lost.

I follow him out to the ledge
where he smokes, loosing
wisdom like ash.

Under smudged skies he coughs, forgets
the model inside at her pose.
Students bang on the window

but he stays, declares
he loves industrial skies.

Like an old master,
he hand mixes pigments
from poison, chemical dust,

paints his studio   sky colored
so he can sit all night and brood

until dawn, when he can stand
on Manayunk Bridge to render

what's dark, what glows.

NIGHT FLOWERS

The model has ruddy skin.
He angles his jaw without regret,
juts his cheekbones outward.
Here anyone might take a swing

but, unconcerned, he gazes out
beyond our circle of easels and arms
that swipe and stroke with brushes.

He is beautiful and survives, old dancer.
For years we've painted him
in life class or open studio and
I know he performs flamenco.

We were taught to keep
a distance from the models.
But today he confides of arthritis.
Doctors warn not to pose on hard surfaces.

There's swelling in his knuckles,
cobalt blue shadows.
His could be boxers' hands or
painters' hands, like mine,
which tire and twitch.

I wish he could pose as he once did,
wrists snapped to the rafters, spine arched,
but as he mounts the model's stand
his palms wilt like night flowers.

PAPER

At dawn   I dive
into a stack of Arches
hot press, 180 lbs
10 dollars apiece
off-white sheets.

The best part is
folding. Palms press
unbroken surface
into a sharp spine.

I center the ruler
to keep pressure even
while fibers give in.
The best part is
tearing   nubbly seams.

A panel the span of my arms
will accept landscape, even
beg for it.

I picture
lemon fields, a series
of etchings, mud
under the toes of swaggering women.

Downstairs, growls,
no cereal in this house. When
will I drive them to school? I reach

for the door but

the best part is
stacking   leaf upon leaf of
buttery space   laid out
still warm

from my hands.

PAINTING WITH COLOR–BLIND SON

Sprawled in my studio, he sorts through
tubes of aurelian and cobalt blue, then asks
which I use.

Violet for undertones, I tell him,
yellow ochre for his skin.

Grabbing a brush, he digs in my paints, tries
two strokes then returns to his
black ink gestures on rice paper.

I try to paint him at the mirror, whistling,
tracking the curl of his tongue.
Corn silk hair, he stares at
ears pale as moths,
eyes like aggies fallen
to the bottom of the bowl.

Feathering quick strokes, I
tilt his portrait towards him.

What does he note, my boy
who doesn't see colors?

He nods, turns back
to his ink, dips a brush, whips up

a thousand wings.

NO MISTAKES IN ART

NOT FORBIDDEN

A quince breaks into bloom
outside the school

where I sketch
(between classes)

trying to capture its tangle of citrus,
its rooted stance

against brick walls,
which can't contain children

from chanting, jostling
down stairwells, proclaiming

poems,
        vivid and delicious.

GIRL ON FIRE

You wrap yourself in poems.
Graffiti snakes around your neck,
wrists and fingers inked
in a tangled bible.

You jangle windows, rattle doors,
taunt the guards, who are armed.
Silence you can't permit
and you stir your pride

until it flies off towards my arms
filled with journals and books,
perhaps strong enough
to quench the god of anger.

Beautiful, pierced child,
spark this room with your burning tongue.
Climb a rope of your own sinew.
Who could not see you within these flames?

INSPIRE

Lanky bodies array themselves
motionless in seats.
Here perch their teenage selves
their childhood selves,
                        alert
beneath maroon shirts
and stoic expressions.
No twitch of smile,
no weakness.

If they balk
fights won't grow full-blown. Guards
poise in corners.

so we write of
the savor of cookies or Cokes,
skateboard speed.

I coax poems, encourage
truth in voice, in recall.
One boy laughs
telling his account of arrest,
leaping roofs and fences,
finally cornered.

Almost a brag.
No one snickers.
But each follows with a story
fiercer than the next.
Each face arranged as a mask.
I do the same, mute

my expressions but
something clenches in me,
some talon grip

when one child shares
her apology poem to the man
who beat her, her sorrow
that some fierce flying
within her
            inspired him.

SPIT

This is a safe room
of sorts, door ajar
so the guard in the hallway can
heed disruptions.
In the corner another guard
flicks eyes from me
to a teen
to another teen, gauges
tension of shoulders, of fists
gripping pencils
    I've given
which they must return
when class ends
    because pencils are weapons.

But how will they write
weapon poems,
witness poems,
hard-to-believe poems
which must be believed.

Listen (I urge)
to what's in your heart, spit
(is the term) write, recite
and next week when you return

we'll all spit.

PORTRAIT

Sketching at the zoo,
we'd rough in the forms of giant turtles
like tilting boulders.

Beside the lion cage
we'd glide sticks of charcoal
to imitate their prowl.

Once the pride male leapt to a ledge
across from the tiger on his ledge.
Neither flinched.
What passed between them?

Or between us
that last day teaching
before you got so sick?

Our students sat rapt
while you demonstrated
how to sketch portraits
with a loose grip.

You wavered, nearly fell
but gestured away
my help

and eyed me, as if
from a long distance.

TWO ARTISTS

My granddaughter sketches us
waving elegant, brush-like fingers
under a cobalt fantasy sky.
It's free of turbulence.
Her stylized sun sends hard-edged rays
over a lime green landscape where we stand, almost
identical,
although I'm taller.

She draws us both
in long red dresses with lemon hair
although mine, in reality, is graying.
Her box of markers is limited,
no complex hues from the natural world,
but next time I'll bring more.

At this stage, she's fascinated
by full-on versus profile perspectives.
Laboring over noses at odd angles, she draws
two breasts on the right side of our bodies.
It's very Cubist, or like a cave painting, I say.
You descend from a long line of stylists.

She can scratch, scribble, invent
whatever she wants
even when she ultimately tears it up, alarmed
when our heads migrate
too far from our bodies.

There are no mistakes in art, she declares
as I place more paper before her.

FLEET

Shrieking, they scamper,
part-chipmunk, part-squirrel.

They climb to the top of the slide then waver (I gasp)
but they seek this moment, this danger.
Balanced
            for one supreme moment
                                    they barrel down,
fierce children
who whirl in light,
in cooling weather.

I labor to breathe through many porous layers.

Once I climbed bleachers
on a day this bright
with my father,
entranced by drumbeat, sport, colored flags.
Whooping and cheering, we jumped, sparks.
I pressed against my father, shivered.

The air is that shivery now.
And who can I tell,
not my fleet grandchildren, racing away

in their necessary leaping.

FULCRUM

I can rough in
a sketch   with
loose lines across a page   map
the territory   then trust
my vantage point.

On my first night's stay
with my son and his new wife
I zigzag, half-drunk, led
by marigolds in jam jars,
bright little arrows strewn
through the house.

In corners, mint pots
wait   to be planted.
Carafes cool
on a woven cloth.

Some of art is
focus, where to
brush in the highlights
to pull   the eye.

Maybe the fulcrum is
my son's brief smile
or the point   where her hand
strokes the dog curled
beside her on the green striped chair.

CHICKENS

I try to depict the farmhouse and woods,
try to hold then release
                              into brushstrokes
barking fox cubs, dappled light,
trilling chickens beside my son's red coop.

I don't trust the fowl.
Last week a young rooster (gorgeous, yellow plumed)
launched himself at my son's wife,
had to be fought off.

She did it herself.
Threw her shirt over his head and
grabbed a branch.
                              .
Now she shows me her clematis
clinging to the coop
                              and the new door
planed from a tree felled by last year's hurricane.

I'd been frantic.
Called them every hour.

The chickens lost their bearings then.
Half refused the coop
                              and huddled all night in the
bushes.

VELOCITY

Wrens vie for space
where seed funnels down
through a hole in the feeder.

They orbit the pole as though drunk.
Light bodies ping-pong out
then snap back.

Why do they joust?

I've seen three perch together
for long minutes
on the feeder's lip

until a cardinal sweeps in, imperious
and they flit off.
Do they sense his vibration before he appears?

Why do I linger, transfixed?
Don't I know all this,
how instinct works?

Or maybe it's simply
velocity, how air
opens up.

REHEARSAL

Two serene young women stand
arm in arm   like clouds set loose
above a field. In such light

we once danced,
singing nursery songs.

This will be a fine wedding.
I grasp
the other mother.

We should have
sky colored dresses   for ourselves.
Don't we deserve them?
Haven't we mothered
such vastness?

AS WITNESS, AS ECHO

FLAME

Window to window, I track her
calligraphy, longing to stroke
where her edges disappear.

In the hedges, flame tail,
plumed fox tail,
thick for winter.

Inside to outside, I seesaw,
spirit spinning,
glass between us.

Oh, to paint her
nesting in the sandbox, unruffled
by car horn, leaf crunch, dog bay.

Bounding to a berm, she poses
queenly, notes the breeze, the branches,
light shifts in the house

where I'm at watch.
And the moment I take up my camera
she's gone.

LANDSCAPES

If you paint
slowly

and breathe with
restraint, a hilltop

may shift to
a more comfortable

position. You may see
shadows

bend, retrieving
fruits blown

too early
from their arms.

The place you
return to

will surprise you.
At dusk

it crowds with birches
discussing

weather. Streams
reroute overnight.

You plant your feet
among whispering maples and

pray no sharp wind
blows this over.

AUTUMN, SENSATE

I swivel bright orange peppers in a jug,
an attempt at arrangement
but they rebel,
angling towards the window.
Dropping my paintbrush, I rip
failed sketches into bits.

Why must every still life
turn into another search for bounty?

Sunday family rides, wanting
roadside pumpkins, bright mums.
Hours of driving, my sisters
wailing and thumping in back,
mother cursing.

Our car careens, stops short.
This, before seatbelts, her arm
whops my chest, protective.
I don't flinch.

Why was it important,
this long search for cider and corn,
no one speaking?

Now I cradle the pepper heads,
swivel their stalks.
Riotous, they flame like jewels.

BLUER THAN SKY

Morning glories flourish on a fence,
unafraid of evening,
which will come. *O*

how beautiful, Mother says, then
submits to another
coughing spasm before
withdrawing into cool rooms.

Frantically, I sketch
like a child hurrying home, clutching
an imperfect
clay ashtray   hand-shaped.

For hours I try
to render this garden, these blue
pale petals that refuse to wilt.

STILL LIFE

Blood oranges wait
on the sideboard.
Painting their shadows   keeps them
in place, not
scurrying, not
making a break for it.

Cherry branch   in a vase
flings out an arm.

Everything fits
on this ten by twelve canvas:
peach
on the cutting board,
twisted gray dishcloth, table
edge.

PORTRAIT AT 87

Dad sits near the glass door
which illuminates
the bony ridges and wings
of his head.

His gaze flicks
to his inner voices
and sometimes to me, silent daughter
wielding a brush.

I try to record
his cloudy eyes, now sepia
as in old photos,
framed and safe.

His soul gets squirrelly if confronted head-on
so I set up my easel to the side
for a three-quarter classical view.

The Masters knew much about portraiture.
Dürer painted onto the orb
of his own eye

a miniature window
so that all these years later
we can peer in.

FULL WEIGHT

Since my parents' departure
their rooms
have a weight
as though a thousand invisible balloons
inhabit them
and slowly deflate,
as happens after parties.

Their souls loll about
ankle deep,
tripping me up
as I move through their apartment.

I long for what echoes, what lingers
in closets and drawers.
Chanel No. 5, Eau de Nuit
attract   repel
like magnets lined up pole to pole,
resistant,
unable to give solace.

Is this what happens?
My soul resists
                their souls
and now must
drift on its own?

TURNING THINGS OVER

A neighbor floats into my kitchen
as I scour pots and polish silver.
I'm shocked to see her
smooth cheeked, unwrinkled.

Your mother never calls, she complains
then offers updates:
one of her children married, one skis.
One won't speak to the others.

I conjure my own voices,
mother warning from beyond:
Tell nothing, not troubles, not joys.
People only want to jabber on.

I upend the salt,
scattering luck
then hurry to brush away crystals
before the forks and knives corrode.

My corporeal father fiddles with radio dials.
He offers this wisdom:
Sometimes there's static,
sometimes it's clear.

This time of year
souls congregate near the river,
release obligations with both hands

while crickets whir.

PLEIN AIR

In a suburban park we're
vertical lines beside easels.

We wave arms in the air, as though
rehearsing a grand orchestra.

Through cupped fingers, we note
azure leaves, azaleas, purpling path to

a toddler releasing a red ball,
a snap-jaw who tugs on his leash, snaps back.

I punctuate what vibrates:
dashes and child twirl, chattering squirrels

while you unspool darks
that simmer below.

How long will we last
as witness, as echo?

SHARP, LUMINOUS

I help my grandchild stack
plastic blocks   into careful piles
she knocks down.

Impartial, she is
delighted
to erect or vanquish
towers.

Red, green, orange   scatter
over carpets and fields with
percussive pops.

Leaning right, she topples
overcome.
My arms brace
to catch her   but the point is
to be a tower
                falling, rising
while your bright bits fly out.

Five times, ten times   she repeats
until breathless, draped
over my lap.

I'm a net, a canvas   stretched
to the contours, beginning

to question all I've been:
careful sketches, brushstrokes.

Someone should have warned me

of this fierce child who

strokes my cheek, gazes about with
sharp, luminous eyes.

THE TROUBLE WITH SELF-PORTRAIT

Starts with the mirror.
Whose face is this   memory sees
softer, more wide-eyed?

I blame the angle flattening
every feature:
brow, cheek bones, lips held
taut in concentration.

The trouble with self-portrait is
admitting what has
slackened.

You study an image
part you   part remembrance
until newness fills in
around your
wavering: bird feathers,
bursts of flowers,

all the things
                    you haven't said.

ACKNOWLEDGEMENTS

I thank several mentors for their wise attention to these poems: the late A.V. Christie, Nathalie Anderson and Fran Quinn. Thanks to poets Alyson Adler and Katherine Barham for their insights. It was a pleasure to work with Nick Courtright and Trista Edwards at Atmosphere Press. I am grateful for my wonderful friends and family, especially my sisters, children and grandchildren. Love to my husband, David, for his love and support.

I gratefully acknowledge the editors from the following journals and publications in which some of these poems first appeared:

Beautiful Cadaver Project: *Is It Hot in Here or Is It Just Me?* (Anthology): *Sharp, Luminous*

Cagibi: *Map*

East Coast Ink: *Stealing Colors*

Four Quarters Magazine: *Studio*

Ishaan Literary Review: *Girl on Fire* and *Paper*

Moonstone Press: *Camera Obscura* (chapbook) in which the following poems appeared: *Sketching Itself, Optics, Life Class, Studio, Paper, Painting with Color-Blind Son, Fulcrum, Chickens, Autumn, Sensate, Bluer than Sky, Landscapes, Sharp, Luminous, The Trouble with Self-Portrait*

Rockvale Review: *Full Weight*

Rogue Agent: *Green (portions)*

ABOUT ATMOSPHERE PRESS

Atmosphere Press is an independent, full-service publisher for excellent books in all genres and for all audiences. Learn more about what we do at atmospherepress.com.

We encourage you to check out some of Atmosphere's latest releases, which are available at Amazon.com and via order from your local bookstore:

Big Man Small Europe, poetry by Tristan Niskanen
In the Cloakroom of Proper Musings, a lyric narrative by Kristina Moriconi
Lucid_Malware.zip, poetry by Dylan Sonderman
The Unordering of Days, poetry by Jessica Palmer
It's Not About You, poetry by Daniel Casey
A Dream of Wide Water, poetry by Sharon Whitehill
Radical Dances of the Ferocious Kind, poetry by Tina Tru
The Woods Hold Us, poetry by Makani Speier-Brito
My Cemetery Friends: A Garden of Encounters at Mount Saint Mary in Queens, New York, nonfiction and poetry by Vincent J. Tomeo
Report from the Sea of Moisture, poetry by Stuart Jay Silverman
The Enemy of Everything, poetry by Michael Jones
The Stargazers, poetry by James McKee
The Pretend Life, poetry by Michelle Brooks
Minnesota and Other Poems, poetry by Daniel N. Nelson
Interviews from the Last Days, sci-fi poetry by Christina Loraine

ABOUT THE AUTHOR

A painter and teacher, Cathleen Cohen founded the We the Poets program at ArtWell, an arts education non-profit for children in Philadelphia (www.theartwell. org). She was the 2019 Poet Laureate of Montgomery County, PA. Cohen received the Interfaith Relations Award from the Montgomery County PA Human Rights Commission and the Public Service Award from National Association of Poetry Therapy. Her artwork is on view at Cerulean Arts Gallery (www.ceruleanarts. com).

9 781636 495620